Voyager
Passport C ™

ISBN 978-1-4168-0365-2
206009

Printed in the United States of America   10 11 12 13 14   BANG   9 8 7 6 5 4 3

One Hickory Centre • 1800 Valley View Lane, Suite 400 • Dallas, Texas 75234 • 1-888-399-1995

Table of Contents

Jobs

Teaching Is a Good Job 1

Ted's Job 2

Do You Like to Cook? 3

Going to the Beach

Joe and Bea at the Sea 4

Mice at the Beach 5

Things to Do at the Beach 6

Problem Solvers

Nature's Toothbrush 7

Ouch! A Bee Sting 8

Leon's Pen 9

A Long Bus Ride 10

KK Warms Up 11

Pied Piper 12

Timed Passage 13

Timed Passage 14

Word List 15

Fluency Practice

 Read the story to each other.

 Read the story on your own.

 Read the story to your partner again. Try to read the story even better.

 Questions? Ask your partner two questions about the story. Tell each other about the story you just read.

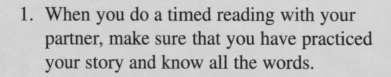

Timed Reading

1. When you do a timed reading with your partner, make sure that you have practiced your story and know all the words.

2. When you are ready, tell your partner to start the timer.

3. Read carefully, and your partner will stop you at 1 minute. When you stop, mark your place.

4. Count the total number of words you read.

5. In the back of your Student Book, write the number of words you read and color in the squares on your Fluency Chart.

6. Now switch with your partner.

Teaching Is a Good Job

Teaching may seem like all fun, but it is hard work as well. Teachers go to school for many years. Some teachers may teach just one thing, and some may teach many things. Your teacher can teach you to read and write and how to do math. She may teach Greek or about life on a beach or on a tall peak. She may teach you how to play ball or skip rope. She can help you if you are in need. Be sweet to your teacher and learn so you can reach your dreams. One day you may teach!⑩⓪

Ted's Job

Ted needed a job. He went over the things he liked best. He liked to bike, but biking was not a job. He liked to hike, but hiking was not a job. He also liked to ride horses, but riding was not a job. What could he do? He sat gazing, "There must be a job for me." Then he had an idea. He biked up the street to a place he had seen and talked to a man. He had the best new job! He would work at a camp teaching biking, hiking, and riding to kids each day.⁽¹⁰⁰⁾

Do You Like to Cook?

Do you like cooking? You could be a chef, but you must prepare before your pals can dine.

First, there is planning what to make. Will you be grilling fish or chopping things for stew? Then, you must do the shopping for your meal. Getting all the things you need is a must! Next, you will be prepping to cook. Get all the pots and pans you will use and start cutting and chopping. Now you can cook without stopping.

Yum! Grilled fish with green beans and a cake topped with jam make a fine meal. You are a chef! ⓘ⁰⁰

Joe and Bea at the Sea

"Here we go," said Bea. Joe and Bea were running into the sea to swim.

"Stop," said Joe, "I see a crab. Look how small he is."

Bea looked. "He is not much bigger than a pea. He has lost his shell," she said.

"We must find him a new shell," said Joe. They looked on the beach. Soon a wave swept one in. They helped the crab into the new shell, and he was safe. "Yea," said Bea. "Now we can play."

But Joe said "No." A wee crab was on his toe!

"Here we go again," said Bea.⑩⓪

Mice at the Beach

Joe and Bea came home from the beach and told their pet mice what fun it was. Soon the mice had a chance to slip out of their cage to go see the sand and waves. They crept up to the edge of the water. Bam! A wave swept them out with the tide and then back on the sand. They rubbed the sand off their faces and saw a huge clam. It snapped. They ran home at a fast pace. At last they were safe in their space. "The beach was not for us. We are mice not fish!" ⑩⓪

Things to Do at the Beach

Do you daydream about going to the seashore? Quit dreaming! Put your things in a backpack and go. It will be fun. Here are some ideas from a travel notebook of fun things to do and things you should know:

1. Put on sunscreen or you will get a sunburn!
2. Look for seashells.
3. Play a game like football in the sand with your pals.
4. Sit in the sunshine and write postcards to someone.
5. Go for a swim and overtake a wave.
6. Take some snapshots of your trip to the seaside!

What tips can you add?⑩⓪

Nature's Toothbrush

How can you brush your teeth when you don't have a toothbrush? Eat an apple! An apple is sometimes called "nature's toothbrush."

Apples are hard and don't stick to your teeth. When you bite into an apple, it cleans food off your teeth.㊸

Try using "nature's toothbrush." Eat lunch. Feel your teeth. Then eat an apple. Feel your teeth again. Can you tell that they are cleaner after eating the apple? The crunchy apple scrubs your teeth!

Ouch! A Bee Sting

What should you do if a bee stings you? First, wash the area with cold water. Then hold ice on it. Did you know food could help too?㉘

Place a slice of onion on the sting. It will make the pain go away. Squeeze the onion to put onion juice on the area. You'll smell like an onion, but you'll feel better!

Leon's Pen

Leon lived a long time ago. Leon liked to write stories, but he didn't like stopping to dip his pen in a bottle of ink.㉕

First, Leon tried to use less ink. He stopped crossing the *t*'s in his stories. This idea didn't work. Many of the words were too hard to read.㊾

Next, Leon filled a big pail with ink. He put the pail on a shelf. He put one end of a thin hose in the pail. He put the other end on his pen. Ink filled Leon's pen. He could write without stopping now.㊾

Leon's dog Pup ran by. She bumped the shelf, and the pail of ink fell on the floor. What a mess! Leon cleaned up the spill. He got out his small bottle of ink and dipped in his pen. Maybe it was not such a bad way to work after all.

A Long Bus Ride

Derek and his father sat down on the bus. The bus drove slowly. It stopped by tall buildings. It slowly turned the corner. The bus drove by more tall buildings. Soon Derek's father fell asleep. Then Derek fell asleep. The bus stopped and started. Derek slept. Derek's father slept.⁴⁹

Derek dreamed he and his father swam with ducks in a lake.

Derek woke up. He saw a lake and ducks. "Dad, where are the tall buildings? Where is the city?"

Derek's father looked out the window. He smiled and said, "It's the park. You woke up just in time. Let's go feed the ducks."

KK Warms Up

KK Gregory played in the snow with her brother. They built a fort out of snow. KK wore a coat and gloves to keep warm, but snow kept going up the sleeves of her coat. KK's arms were soon cold and wet.

KK went inside to warm up. She needed something to cover the space between her sleeves and her gloves. KK's mom helped her sew some warm fabric into a little sleeve. It fit on KK's arm and her hand. It had one hole for her thumb to go through, but it didn't have fingers like a glove. KK put the two little sleeves on under her coat and over her gloves. She went back out to play in the snow.(122)

Pretty soon, snow started getting under the little sleeves and onto her hands. KK went back inside. She made two new, smaller sleeves. This time she put them on under her gloves. KK went back outside. Her hands and arms stayed warm and dry.

KK knew she had a good idea. She called the little sleeves Wristies® and made them for her friends. Everyone loved them. KK started selling Wristies to stores and on TV. KK Gregory had solved her problem with a winning idea.

Pied Piper

The town of Hamelin had a problem. It had rats. Rats lived everywhere in the town.

The mayor called the people together. "What can we do to get rid of the rats?" he asked.

"I can help you," said a man in a long coat. "I am the Pied Piper. If you pay me money, I will get rid of all the rats in Hamelin." The mayor promised the Pied Piper the money if he got rid of the rats.

The Pied Piper began to play his flute. He walked down the streets of Hamelin. Rats came out of holes, houses, stores, and garbage cans. They followed the Pied Piper.⑪⑩

The Pied Piper walked to the river. The rats jumped into the river.

"All your rats are gone," said the Pied Piper. "Now you can pay me."

The mayor laughed. He would not pay the piper.

The Pied Piper began to play his flute again. He walked down the streets of Hamelin. Boys and girls came out of houses. They followed the Pied Piper.

The Pied Piper walked to a mountain. He hid the children. "Now you will pay me!" said the piper.

No More Spoon Washing

Every day Marta Goodin fed her cat. She used a spoon to scoop food from a can. Then she washed the cat food spoon. Marta did not like washing the messy spoon.㉜

Marta asked her grandmother for help. Together they made dough. They made it into the shape of a spoon and baked it in the oven.

Marta used the dough spoon to scoop food out of the can. Then she broke the spoon into bits and put the bits in the cat's bowl too. The cat ate the cat food, but it did not eat the spoon.

Marta made more dough. This time, she added some cat food to the dough. She tried again, and the cat ate its food and the spoon. No more spoon washing for Marta!

Mia's Lunch

Mia wanted lunch. She got out cheese and tomato. She'd make a cheese and tomato sandwich.

"Mama, where is the bread?" Mia said.

"We're all out," said her mom.

Mia put her head in her hands. What could she eat? Then she had an idea. She'd put cheese and tomato on a bun.

"Mama, where are the buns?" Mia said.

"We're all out," said her mom.

Mia walked around the room. Then she had an idea. She'd put cheese and tomato on crackers. But they were out of crackers too.⑨⓪

No bread, buns, or crackers! How could Mia make lunch?

Mia looked in the refrigerator. She looked on the shelf. She found many things. Then she had an idea.

Mama helped Mia cut a potato into thick, round slices. Mama fried the slices in a pan. When they were cool, Mia put cheese and tomato on one potato slice. She put another slice on top. It made a good lunch.

Word List

there	would
each	some
she	like
running	time
taping	into
about	look